Vivaldi
in Early Fall

Vivaldi
in Early Fall

POEMS BY
JOHN ENGELS

Athens
The University of Georgia Press

Set in 10 on 12 point Monticello type
Printed in the United States of America

Library of Congress Cataloging in Publication Data

Engels, John.
  Vivaldi in early fall.
  I. Title.
PS3555.N42V5   811'.54   80-24571
ISBN 0-8203-0543-X
ISBN 0-8203-0552-9 (pbk.)

for Gail

*"Swetenesse of this paradyse hath
ye ravysshed; it semeth ye slepten
apart from al diseses, so kyndeley
is your herte therein ygrounded."*
> Thomas Usk, *The Testament of Love*

The publication of this book is supported by a grant from the National Endowment for the Arts, a federal agency.

Acknowledgments

I wish to thank the Vermont Council on the Arts, Yaddo, the Virginia Center for the Creative Arts, the John Simon Guggenheim Memorial Foundation, and the administration of St. Michael's College, especially Dean Vernon Gallagher, all of whom in one way or another have contributed to my support during the time this book was being written. I am especially grateful to Hayden Carruth, David Huddle, and Mark Strand for their help and friendship.

I also wish to acknowledge the following publications in which poems from this volume first appeared. *The Agni Review:* "Adam Signing" (here as the first poem in section I), © 1979 by *The Agni Review. Antaeus:* "After Thirteen Years," "Muskrat," "Saying the Names," "The Mothwing, Ice at Dawn," "The Electric Fence Game," "Shark," "Partridge." *Black Warrior Review:* "Port Cities," "Poem on My Birthday," "The Cold in Middle Latitudes" (which is also a Pushcart Prize selection for 1980), "Joyce Vogler in 1948." *Choomia:* "The Fragonard, the Pietà, the Starry Sky." *Chowder Review:* "In Panama," "Mudtrapped." *Claymore:* "Great Grandmother." *Columbia:* "Naming the Animals," "Revisiting the Grave." *The Georgia Review:* "The Harbor." *Harper's:* "Bullhead," "The Disconnections," "For Mozart, from the Beginning." *Iowa Review:* "Vivaldi in Early Fall," © 1977 by the University of Iowa. *The Nation:* "The Geese," "Van Gogh Prophesies the Weathers of His Death." *New England Review:* "At Night on the Lake in the Eye of the Hunter," "Artesian." *New Letters:* "Earth Tremor" (here as the first poem in section II). *Ploughshares:* "Thinking of the Garden." *Salmagundi:* "Mahler Waiting," "The Crows." *Sewanee Review:* "The Guardian of the Lakes at Notre Dame," © 1979 by the University of the South. *Virginia Quarterly Review:* "Bog Plants," "Dreaming of the Natural History Museum."

J. E.

Contents

I

Adam Signing

Here in the cool, birdlit realms,
his breath drawn out into the sky
which more than himself has come
to wish to breathe, he stands

on the verge of the cliff, far short
of where the impulse to go on
might much have lessened; and he stares
down on the Garden's silences,

not seeing her, who—in that instant
risen from the light of the yellow
seedling grasses—looks up at him
and cannot catch his eye or call out to him,

somehow signal, finding herself to be
still faint and tremulous of voice,
the soft flesh of her hands
still taking place; and sees him make

suddenly, without warning, into the milky air
the difficult signs for love, *for*
danger, *as well as the simpler one*
for flight, *not even thinking to be seen*

or answered, and therefore
gesturing so swift, so gorgeously complex
into the calyx of the sky
that she—looking into the rushed

dance of his hands—in that first,
most urgent measure of
these silences, could not
well follow him.

Thinking of the Garden

This is the kind of night
on which Yuan Chen cried out
to his dead wife, *when one
dreams of another, are both
aware of it?* the moonlight
blackening his bed, the ice roaring
in the great rivers
of Honan. From such a night

Adam himself awoke, knowing none of this
had ever been, opened his eyes
onto the glorious mess of the contingent,
propped himself on one elbow,
and without astonishment gave names
to the *bee-orchid*, the *giraffe*.

*

If, when I awaken,
I am lying beside you,
I reach out to touch
the warm ridge of your spine.
It is how I try to tell you
there are imbalances, the end,
the ineloquent function,
begins to demonstrate itself.

The silence between us,
the frightening stars, the great Bear
riding the horizon, even

the darks of the farther lawns
are nothing: I wish to tell you

it is finished,
knowing fully the lie, knowing
if there is this silence,
it is measureable,
nor does the need lessen.
For now I touch you with my hands
that are hands. Later
the dust will not forget
what it has loved.

The Garden

A river bank,
outside a walled garden. Later
the interior of the garden. Later still
a rose-plot, surrounded by
a hedge, inside
the larger garden. Its single garnishment,
a great sun, powerfully
shines. Unhappily

this garden is empty, though
from time to time a bird sings
and there is a shower of warm rain.
But to the north, far to the north,
it is beginning, the snow falls
and hardens, and all the white beasts
begin to wander south. And it is then, just then,

that from nowhere, at the very center
of the garden, there appears
someone for the single purpose
of noticing the slight
shortening of days, the bare
chilling of the air in the first
lights of morning: *Love*,
Beauty, *Bravery* take shape

in his smile, though for the moment
he gives way to the first
prophetic fancy, dreams
of a scarlet sun the size of a rosebud,

unfolding and unfolding
from its locked center.
And when in time the first snow blows
over the walls, he makes it out to be
no more than a cloud of petals
from some blooming tree. Such then
the scene, and such the character,
who finally sleeps, and is crushed
by the great ice coming over him,
his bones, the whole time,
warm in the pious dream, the body
of the earth hollowing beneath him;
and the garden, of course, no garden at all,
as if it had never been,
and all time spilled for nothing.

The Guardian of the Lakes at Notre Dame

I cannot any longer bring to mind
the name of the ancient, hated Brother
who patrolled the lakes at Notre Dame,
and ran the kids off, waving an old gun
from the far shore, shouting in a voice
that from one hundred yards away
was dangerous as sword blades.

Retired to guard the lakes, the old man did;
and for him to wake up was to most powerfully insist
that turtles be troubled merely to feed,
herons to fly, snakes to dream of toads.
Himself the caring center of all careless
natural grace, at last he died;
the lakes were fished.

There is perhaps
something to say in favor of old men
who raise the guardian arm and voice against
the hunting children—who but lately come
to Paradise, pursue
the precedent beast unto its dumb destruction,
and persist.

And surely the sky came more and more to seem
like the dark-enclosing vault
of the dead box-turtle's shell. Perhaps he thought
to cry against the children was like love,
love being often in rebuke of innocence.
In all event they plundered the far shore,

and he waved his gun, and shouted out at them
Go home go home! in fierce stern order that
they might be made to see, how, in the end
the bellowing angel raises up his fist,
and how that is to be
forfeit of name in the memory of men.

Dreaming of the Natural History Museum

Today I wake up and recall
of the entire dream only
the ceremonial ochres
of the skull of the Miami brave,
the pickled bull snake in its jar, its pallid
coils, the gold pendulum, big
as my head, that swung forever around the red
X of center, proving the planet and therefore
Indiana truly turned.

But most of all, most coldly legible,
something of stone, the great
whorl of the six-foot fossil nautiloid,
balanced against the north museum wall, ready
to topple at my least
step. And that is all—
coil of snake, round hollow of bone, circling
of plumb bob, and the stone shell,
taller than the child it might have crushed,
spinning in upon the perfect
and revolute center,

everything in memorable stance, everything
at dead center, the old dusts
in plain array. Today
I awaken and look
into the red bullseye that my son
has painted on the bathroom mirror. I see
myself, which is to say
whatever there is to say of dream,

of language, of necessity—
the waking eye dead center and each waking day
the same slow, enormous ceremony of retrieval;
however the need maintains, however
the elusive, agile shapes may grow
from the casual shelter of my bones, I know

the recollection of matter
is the suicide of angels,
the last giving-over
of the dead.

Mudtrapped

for John Reiss

One time I waded far out in a lily slough
on the Clyde's backwaters, and my boots
caught in powerful suctions of black ooze,

and I sank, until the water, at my chin,
stopped rising on me: something held me up.
I drank warm air, and well I might have stayed

forever there, deep-rooted in the bottom mucks
like some enormous lily; but my friends came,
I was rooted out, dragged in.

I think if it's true the black night sometimes
swallows us like that, the planet softens, liquefies,
tries to draw us in to where we drown,

it is to the grace and rule of counterpoise applies,
or so Desire requires us to believe,
fearing as we do Love's natural buoyancies

are no true balance to the pulling-down.

11

Bog Plants

Thirty years later the night is the purple flush
the pitcher plant's throat.
Sitting alone, "which is the beginning of error,"
I think of the flflower itself, the snake-mottled
belly of leaf that bulged from the loam near the hose;
and the clawed pads of the flytrap that never mistook
my probing with stems for the brunt
of the entering beetle. And the sundews I moved
from the Berrien bogs tto grow
in the house's north shade,
in late June, in those days when the skies
over South Bend were burning, burning, and if
there ever was rain it came down as a power of light.

I think of the light: as my eye today
unfocuses, suffers no clarity, then
it blurred and recoiled from the sun on the white
east side of the house, the house giving back
such dazes of light, so blinding, I turned
to stare into the shades of the ell, the damp
corner of bog plants, the other blindness
coming over me: and consequent
nightmare—

My body at rest in the white, cool soils of the bed,
my head foursquare on the pillow, the sheets
so neat at my chin that merely to stir
was to trouble the whole
house, its bordering acres,
I dreamed the beginning of error:

I was thorax of wasp, the impervious
chitins of beetle, carapace, husk,
a blurring, corrodible heart,
the bone sour in the belly's
vigorous juices. And there
was the slow, large, convulsive gulp of the dark.

Joyce Vogler in 1948

That beautiful pale girl with yellow hair
than whom I shall not other love, nor half so much,
stood with me waiting for the Portage Bus,
hands in her pockets, collar up against the wind,

and grinned at me, and laughed. But I
was worried: it was late, the bus
was late, or I may
have missed it altogether, and

my mother would be waiting up,
and I would not see this girl again forever;
and that has been
the terrible, slow truth of it, not wish, not love

recalling me to that night when the wind,
sweet with catalpa blossom, swelling
and softening, drifting her yellow hair
across my face, broke sternly on us. Now,

in the monstrous wake of passage, I give up
to no less love than did not understand before
the flesh intent on its own timely bearing.
The night hums crazily with wind and trees,

and birds fly, as if it were full day.
I see her laugh at me. I look away,
I crane to see the whole black empty length
of Portage Avenue—and there, at the end,

is the late, the final bus,
ablaze with yellow light,
just turning out from the billowing night
at the far end of the street; for always

me worried me, though always
I was home in time.

Saying the Names

My name: *John. Norbert,*
my father's; my grandfather's, *William,*
David, my brother. *Margaret, Patricia,*
Julie, Euphrasia,
of the women of my family. Uncles,
James, and *Bill,* and *Vincent.*
Laura, Leon, grandparents. My mother,
Eleanor; Gail, my wife, my

children, *Jessica, David, John,*
Laura and *Matthew;* the dead son,
Philip—all the names
said for the simple saying,
the plain acknowledgment,
always as if my ear were pressed
to the hearts of my people,
my breath warm
on their breasts.

And outside, the nameless formulations
waiting for names:
the sun rising, the lakes,
the still fields filling up with snow,
my whole days filling
with the dull syllables of pulse,
the watch in my breast pocket
louder, more regular, than my heart.

Always, more than anything,
I wish to say the names:

even with my dead before me,
I say the names
into the bright, breathable air,
all the names
of our uncommon time
beating in my tongue,
myself beyond
that possibility,

myself awakening
in the middle of the night, breath
regathering,
the uncommon breath;
and the last loud syllable
of what I take to be
the one great general name I never hear
just dying in the room, just
whistling backward
to the utterance.

Great Grandmother

for N.A.E.

I remember my great grandmother
wanting to die, but old and awake
in her bed in the Nicolet Home

for the Aged.
I did not know her, having come
with my father to stand at the foot of her bed

this one time only. Still,
I wished she were not blind,
and could see the blue Fox River

from her window. The room
smelled of sulfides from the mills,
and the red zinnias we had brought her.

*"Hello, Norb, I'm
old, I want to die!"* She
called me by my father's name. I

cannot recall telling her
my name. I know
I did not want to die,

having as yet
no sense of power
in such a thing.

Revisiting the Grave

for Julie & Dave

The day my mother died, I must
have looked out over the green swell
of Lake Michigan sheeting
high on the beaches;
at the last turn of the surf
pine cones rolled over and over;
the river rolled back
at the breakers; clouds
foaming in.

I must have faced into the long
shudder of wind, trusting
my eyes to the sting
of the sand.
But next day:
utter calm.
I might have believed
the planet had stopped in its turns;
and except that my hand touched the wind-

sanded boles of the pines,
I might not have believed
I had witnessed those risings
of water, the drive
of the sand from the lee
shore. And today
it is calm, and except that my hand
touches this grass, I might not
have believed
enough to endure these powerful

weathers of memory, moving
my hands on the swell
of the green turf, palms
dazzling at the dark
gathers of soil; and my eyes—
for all
their staring to windward, for all
that brunt of the dust
they bore, suffering
no abrasion, offering
no visible evidence.

Naming the Animals

Since spring I've seen two deer,
one lashed to a fender. The other fed
in a clearing on the back slope
of Bean Hill, his big rack still
in velvet. The shot buck bled,

its tongue frozen
to the rusty hood.
But the other, in its simpler stance,
felt merely the delicate itch
of antler skin.

And three does, mildly alert,
cocked ears toward where I watched from
in the hemlocks. I saw, of course,
five deer; but I
count only what by plain necessity of death

or feeding is oblivious to me,
does not watch back.

At Night on the Lake in the Eye of the Hunter

That night, drifting far out
in the center of the lake,
I watched the stars; later
I shone my torch down into the eelgrass
of the perch beds, and saw the fish
stunned into thrills and tremblings of fins.

I shone the torch onto my wet hands,
onto the wet sky-reflecting floorboards
of the boat, then onto the sky itself,
the beam widening, thinning into the white
fabrics of mist. That night

I thought I rode the center of all
the widening brightnesses,
that everything was around me, out
to the mountainous far rimstones
of the circling earth.

Later, by starlight seeing
over the whole blue surface of the lake
trout feeding on mayflies,
seeing the cross and recross
of rise rings, the slow
opening of ripples
from the tiny bright insucks
at center,

I came to think how it might have been
my boat hung there in a net

of light, a cold, translatable fire;
however it may have been,
it was then my light began its long
reach, even now, long afterward, still
rising, widening into the body of the sky,
into the last huge widenesses of the last
meetings of light beyond which I remember this
or not, beyond which
even then fearing my life
I wished to burn.

Bullhead

for Bill Dunlop

Sprawled belly-down on the damp
planks, the breath
squeezed in my chest,
I drift the bait
into the pale moon-shadow of the dock

waiting for the blunt
emergence of bullhead,
his slow surge at the worm, glint
of the small, mucusoid eye,
sluggish black spasm of flesh.

I haul him out,
but he does not die at once:
ugly among fish, poisonous dorsal spine erect,
he endures, he swims in the air
for hours, scrabbles and grunts
in the bucket. I have fished
for more than a hundred nights
hearing that gross croak
from the bucket,
and do not forget, am granted the memory:

in that peculiar sleeplessness
which loves those things which resemble
other things, night
after watery night I have tried
to breathe the inappropriate air,
have wanted to call out into the blackness
beyond the dumb, immediate blackness

that I am about to die and cannot die,
but making so dull a voice of the dull
connatural agony, I writhe to it,
grunting aloud, the hook
of the breath snagged
in my gullet, the tongue
in my mouth like a worm.

Muskrat

When the sky
opens itself to the dank reedy smell
that is the lake at this hour,
and the moon rides in that parting of clouds
for fully a minute,

I glance out at the water
through the cluster of pale evening duns on the screen,
through the moon-lighted dazzle of their wings,
and see the fiery V-shape bearing out
into the shatter of light on the lake,
a slow comet of small flesh,
whiskery with grasses.

A small light of stars
behind the clouds,
room light behind me:
the time comes
for me to try to detach my hand's shadow
and reach out; and therefore,
in this night without true fire,
everything cold, night deepening, the lake deepening,
the deepening clarity of flight
in the wing of the imago,

I raise my arm and the room light flings
the long, articulated shadows of thumb
and finger out
onto the lake, out there,
where, through the cold, adoptive fires

of the cold stone of the fireless moon,
the muskrat swims. It is enough, this time,

to frighten him, to make him dive,
to make me imagine him frantically, smoothly
webfooting down through the rank
blacknesses of lake, his fur trailing light,
his wake starry with bubbles, his body
light with the last, terrified
breath-taking. He dives

into the thickening muds of the lake.
And what remains, what I am left to see,
is the floating scatter of cattails,
and how the black field of the lake
has closed on his small, explainable fire.

The Crows

When it was spring in Wisconsin,
and the roosting crows
screamed every morning from the birches
across the lake, alarmed
at the first, predatory light,

I used to push out from shore
on the little waterlogged raft,
awash to my ankles
and find it possible to believe myself
standing on the still water, over
the dangerous place
where the sand bottom dropped away
into the muds of the springhole.

When it was spring in Wisconsin, and morning,
the nights never far away, and the stars
always preparing to burn in the rising field of the lake,
when it was spring and what I stood on
did not fully bear me up,
and if I could drown or fly or hurl myself
into the left and right of the powerful distances,

I had not sufficiently fathomed
how to believe, intent
always on the instance of morning, the voice
of the crow, the small
shivers of air in the delicate drum
of my bones, the rising
beaked sun. I would stand

on the lake in the jaws of the opening light,
a deepening beneath me, a greater
overhead, the gesture
of my reaching out to either side
a movement of so little extension I might,
but do not remember, have shouted
in anger aloud and heard
in reply my own voice fly at me, back

from the trees of the far shore, the words
jumbled and raucous, prolonged
into warning, back
like the bright alarm
of the sun-greeting voice of the crow.

The Geese

Stepping out onto the back porch
in the early evenings of November,
I hear the hissing, the dumb
unfriendly voices of geese.

But in the mornings, in the cold
decorum of light, its lovely
obligations, I walk
in the crackling garden, scuffing
my boots in the frozen
green hillocks of goose droppings,

shiver and watch the Toulouse geese
parading their coop roof, the goose yard
shining with spread wings. Then
night comes and the moon dims
in a blue web of cloud, and the birches
at the yard's far edge sway
like the white necks of geese;
and each time I feel night as a bird

and myself caught in the warm angle
between wing and body of a bird,
sharing the convulsion of desire it is
to beat down on the stony planet,
and rise, and fly.

Partridge

Eyes frosting over, its shattered beak
polished with new blood,
at my feet lay the partridge
which only an instant before had flushed
from the beech grove and hurtled
whirring low over the winter yard
to come up short against
the brick wall of the house.
I picked it up,

the wings disjointed into a soft sprawl
over my wrists, and felt
through the loose throat-skin the crop
bulging and grainy
with mast. My fingers
grew warm on the barred
breast. It was because
my hands were cold I did it,
though, it is true,
for a moment as I stood there
holding the dead bird,
my fingers warm in the soft down,

it seemed never
to have been otherwise,
that from the beginning
I had found myself
likewise frequent in my yards,
and somehow at my feet
the diffident aspect of a body

abruptly impoverished
and mute, which, living,
I could not find palpable.

The Mothwing, Ice at Dawn

1

Nearly spring, though snow
still blurs the world: no edge
to anything, air brightening
with snow, green cloud

of the willow through
the snow; and at dawn
the plain immanence
of fire, grey

blade of the lake, white stones
of the lake bed, shadows
of birds, of stones, of trees;
the icy breach which is the sky.

2

On the spray of apple twigs,
the chrysalis, pricked
from the elegant, strict sleep,
stirs; and I see,

by the first spasm
of morning light, from the frayed
cocoon the moth emerge,
softly to clamber the red

curtain: great
rosy-grey *crecopia*, uncrumpling

its eyed wings' owlstare
into the room

where I have myself begun to feel
something of what the blood's light
carries of this dumb desire
to fly.

3

I leave her there, cold pulse
of insect blood, walk down
to the shore, step out
onto the puddled meadows

of spring ice. I walk out
beyond the point, the air
pitchy with hemlocks, ice
heaving and widening to either side.

I walk into the clear,
thunderous field of the open lake,
I see the moon
thin in the red underbelly

of the sky; from shore,
a small outcry of dry leaves,
a flicker of blue light
among the pines,

some shiver of wing
instinct in the solitude.

4.

Often, at dawn, in the spring,
I walk far out on the ice; sometimes,
following the long shadows
that I make, I raise my arms,

make wings of shadows; at other times
I reach tremblingly out
over the veined ice,
the light deepening, bright dust

upon my arms, ice hoarding air,
clear dust of light, clear
rosy dust of light, the moon
at such times fragile

in the sky, the sun
just brightening, and overhead
the sky ready to flash
with dawn, everything

on the cold verge of fire, everything cast
of the analogate presences.

5

I come out
onto the barrens of spring ice,
beneath which the lake
is swelling: it is

the current
of the wing. I come out
onto the dangerous spring ice,
and look back

to the far shore, from which
I watch myself look back
upon this figure far out on the ice,
which spreads his arms, lies down

on the watery snow, makes snow-wings, wing-marks,
stares into the sky through the lessening snow,
and sees the bright fields of the air
parting before him; and the dream

is that he is about to climb
the white, uncoiling feather of his breath;
the dream is of how
in the full light of the sky, in full

view of everything, he takes
wing-shape, shape of a huge
trembling moth, feels the wing
throb in his shoulder, sees the sky

brighten in the great, faceted domes
of his eyes, a million suns
rising to meet in the splendor
of one shining, the air

filled with the soft
threshing of wings, the blue
ice of the light swelling,
and warming overhead,

everything shaken
into its separate dusts,
the body at last
bearing the wing which is promised,

though not that it will fly—
old
intolerable exaltation
before things, great eye

of the mothwing, green
opening stone of the earth!

The Cold in Middle Latitudes

1

the first of April, I stand
a little before sunrise
on the porch step, and observe
to the north a sudden
discontinuity of sky. I look

in that first light
at the houses of North Williston.
The morning
withholds itself, there is much in it
of refusal. I note
how it is that the world in early spring
exhales the odor
of damp cellars,

which in fact I have always known,
and of which I have spoken,
nor is this the last of it

2

April, which is to say,
by my measure, some small
equivocal truth about how
everything takes place
at the wrong time.
The black

locusts seem dead, the maples
have come half-alive, and wait.

In my yard, in all the yards
of North Williston, the spring muds
steam—and for the moment

(though I permit it
only for the moment)
something like the sun
takes place. For the moment
all the doors stand open,
this house airing,
readying itself,
by evening
the spring frogs chirping
and roaring from the ditches,
and one which has been hiding there all winter
singing out from the cellar

3

a sullen, invisible cold
breathes from the floorboards.
Warm rain begins

at the exact instant that, in the west,
the sky clears, greens, flares overhead,
that everything becomes
as if I were to breathe at the green
fluent heart of the sea,

and looking up
into the vast mirror of the under-
surface, be
permitted to look back upon
myself; which would be to fail
in these imaginings

4

Perhaps I am in
the wrong place:
over North Williston
in the earliest of skies
the sun dwindles into the knot
and smother of its heart.
And my heart,

as it carries itself in me,
as I have known it to undertake to do
sings out in the seasonal
startlement from hiding, willing

and unwilling to become
nothing, but always
unequal to the one
or other
of it

5

as it turns out,
as I expected that it would,
the sky in this place is no more
than merely about
to deepen, to become snow
which will fall and deepen,

and I have in all this weather-lock not
come to understand how it can be
the body warms
to its own and slight
sea-bearing,

the body, as I
have knowledge of it, wishing
always to rise and to beat down
upon a green and upward-
beating shore; and this,

though I see by the blue
shine of the ice that rises
slowly in the east, though I see
by that true and signatory light,

I have
not fully deserved
this knowledge, have
not used it well

Artesian

1

When, as now,
because the pump has shorted out,
the well is dry,
I am unwilling to believe it,

and a dozen times a day reach out,
twist on the tap, expecting
bright fullnesses of water
to swell up in the pipe,

rush over my hands; instead,
am each time newly startled
by the quick back-hiss of the air
through valves, check-valves

and pressure tank, the unfamiliar,
frightening soft suck
and inbreath of the long,
downdraining pipe.

2

Always, to my conviction,
it is there, bellowing
hundreds of feet
beneath the house,

the river, which has never
to this day gone dry, not even

in the hottest summer, never
in the greatest drought,

though when I lie awake
and listen for it, I
hear nothing, only
from somewhere deep

in the deepest parts
of the cellars of whatever
house I have lived in, slow
tricklings of seepage

into the sumps, at times the slow
trickle and thump
of earbloods: all powers of gathering
to which the heart gives rise.

3

I have not before considered,
but do now,
the downstream rising
of the river. I see

an open, marshy corner
of low meadowland, a cold
upwelling through
schists and serpentines, blue

43

glacial clays and muds, a rust
of water among thickets
of cattail; in the bright
shades of marsh

marigolds, tricklings
through cress and duckweed, falls
of willow, cedar, alder
hells, first

poolings, minnow-
flash, bright
riffling of
streambed, sunlit

caddis flight, first
lucid narrows of
the true
channel (Upstream, vague

issuance, the
inconsiderable
source)

4

I fail, as always, to remember
that what the source does not

give up to me, it shall
exact: again, therefore, and again

I walk down
into the still passage
of the house, stand
at the sink, and turn

the taps wide open: *rush*
of house air down the dry
wellpipe—my very
breath drawn down

the breath of everything
I have ever known to be alive drawn down
out of the dry
silences

into what I have taken to be
the inaudible convulsions of water
deep under
the house, the river

gathered there and howling
through glassy arches
of rock, black flumes
and conduits, and hugely

roostertailing, its voice
the voice I have listened for

my whole and sleepless
life, its light

(if this river were to be light)
what I would all day
and every day awaken to,
see by.

After Thirteen Years

"... looked back from the high hill
on the place I used to live" —Ma Rainey.

As always, it is snowing.
The roof flowers with new ice.
In the house the closets succeed themselves
one on diminishing other
to the tiny locked heart
at center. The names

rise up in me
in little, gathering densities.
It is snowing and the sun is rising
into the dead center of the sky;
and everything is white,
under the snow the rocks, dirt, tree roots:
everything is white.
This late at night

the body yearns
for exactitude in things,
feels the silence
in the creature, waits
to want to sleep.
And at this moment
I begin to hear
the small wings of your heart
beating away;
at this moment
I am thinking of you,
of how softly the snow falls,
what it builds to.
In a little while

47

the sun will tear free
from the white cloud of the earth,
the pines on the hill will stand out
against the whiteness of the hill,
and morning will surge in, and I will see
ice, pines, the derangement of Vermont
into mountains. I will see
the fields of the snow
stretching to beyond the farthest
imaginable north.
I will hear
the doors fly open, and the house
will fill with cold. Ice
will be roaring from the roof.
And I will think how, on such a day,
I held you, only an hour born,
your eyes bruised from the first
blunt stun of the light,
small blood
exulting into smaller voice;

and felt most powerfully
the impersonal separation of bloods,
took you to be, as yet unnamed,
proof of the "short day
and the long shadow,"
perhaps no more
than the bitter duty of seed,
of kinship, perhaps
gift beyond gift, the body

being what it is, weak
on the side which does not
lean upon the world.
As for the rest, you died.

If you had lived you would have come to see
how, wishing to die, the body swells and grows;
have come to be startled
by all the accidents of celebration,
even perhaps have come into the voice
which cannot be startled into celebration;
have come to believe,
as I believe,
that at whatever distance we care to imagine
there is only the pale light without shadows
the snow gives off at night,

only the recollection of your voice,
always as distance, always as a tiny cry
from the deep center of the house,
without much conviction to it
in the way of pain.
I dream
I am alone,

And awaken,
frightened, hearing myself
trying to say one last thing
into the air of Vermont,
whispering to whatever

at that instant might seem to require
recognition, but lacking
a usable breath
to discharge what I, even at that moment,
will consider a duty. There is

a mystery here, something like a memory,
something of the voice's continuities,
that it carries long ways,
but weakly, so that hearing it
is like a memory
of the beauty of a body
recognized and welcomed.
I have been free of it,

but now again come to the recognition: snow
outside, light bursting
from the tips of icicles, cardinals
in scatters of red shadow on the snow:
on such days when I sleep
I hear you, touch you, am touched back,
you come to me rising from where you have been,
walking to me over the snow;
and if I turn
to the touch on my shoulder,
there is no one; thus
the cold center continues to achieve itself,
the world is used up.
I have not understood
how it is my mind

exults into this elaborate,
clamorous voice,
or how it is this voice
has opened itself to me,
or how what has seemed to me
the small, clear distant voice
of all the crying out of all time
I continue to hear
from the locked heart of the house
as if I were myself
among the gathering, celebrative dead,
my blood upon the root.
I do not understand
how I have continued to believe
the named thing breathes,
to name what it is I see,
having named you: Philip, fifth-born,

since the naming I know I have seen you
walking across the field towards the fence,
towards the long reach of the pines
into the white field,
wide-legged on snowshoes, the orange bulge of your pack
the brightest thing north of me;
and it is not from this place
you seem to have left—you are walking away
at precisely that middle distance
at which I begin not to see
you will surely return, hours later,
smelling of wood smoke, your shoes soaked, a glove lost,

51

forgetting to close the door behind you,
the ugly pale cold of the fields
flooding in from behind you.
And I begin not to see

what might have been your eye
encountering the young light
of the fields, your foot
on fresh snow. You are named,
you are recognized: slow course of seed
beneath the snow, vigorous
green sprouting
from the severed parts: all my children,
there is today
a soft down-spinning of snow, this
is for you, I speak to you
into the dead center of the snowing sky:

may another, warmer season yet contain
the voices you have not heard,
the shapes on which your hands
will never rest. For now
there is the slow, cold turn about the center.
Look back from the white field
on the place you used to live.

The Electric Fence Game

1

I walk
through the stupid milling
of cattle, come
to the shining wire and reach out,

not daring to hesitate, trusting
to catch hold in the dead time
between pulses, grasp
and ungrasp in perfect

dumb coincidence the wire,
and find it neutral
in my hand: a game
in which the free hand freely

dances, so long as it
keeps time

2

After the first
and risky taking-hold, everything
is safe enough. I stand
and look out over the calm pastures,

scarcely aware
of how on each side
of the instant of my fist
the blunt stun of the power is licking out

3

But even if I have been wrong
and have caught hold and found
the wire humming and alive,
it is the moment I understand

how all along
I have desired my heart to leap
and leap in the irregular
dark spasm and keep on,

have desired
to give up to the cold
pulse of the wire the lesser
power of my hand

to open itself or not, to splay
out fingers, free itself
of what in love or
other synchronous play

it has chanced freely
to close upon and hold.

In Panama

drunker than all the other times
put together squared,
I stared up at the pale belly
of a stuffed shark
that hung over my head and circled
in the damp light of Panama
like a big and predatory
ceiling fan.

And there was the voice
of some woman at the bar, saying
it had hung there in the exact
same place since the day
her father shot it from the deck
of the fishing boat *Juarez*
in the year of
1931. Later,

with a great far cry of darkness in between,
I saw a man in a checkered hat
stand, brace himself
in a yellow circle of street light,
a voice balloon of huge moths
in a slow swirl above his head,
and knock the brains out
of a dog's skull with
a fragile-looking stick. *Brief
infrigidation of the spirit, black
night:* then
awakened on my way to somewhere

in a car which was not
my car and packed
with a great many people
whom I did not know and a cheerful,
horny mongrel which would not
give up trying to hump my knee,
and at last, on the far side of dark interval,
came to, swimming in the deep water
outside the shark net
at Fort Amador. There are some few

concluding figures, all
significant of lapse, dismemberment
or forfeiture: removing from a large,
struggling hermit crab
its legs; embracing
a horribly receptive
toilet bowl; finding I had lost
one shoe and was leaving
bloody footprints on a white rug:

all of it a pristine
radiance of discontinuity,
most hindering
to concoction.

For it has not escaped me
how there is something willful
about all this sweaty effort
at retrieval, this immoderate concern

for whatever locks itself
into some spasm or frenzy
of the brain by custom given over to
dismal conjuration
of the least moth
of the soul, and in the end

I neither sing nor sigh
but am made morose,
permit to rise
these recollections of
the body's most crude
natural heats,

merely recount here
how it happens, and to
me, and
all the time.

Shark

I step into this memory
as if I have come into being a foot from myself,
the road diminishing behind me, and ahead
Marseilles; and I am walking
back from somewhere in late afternoon,

the sea blue as a flax field to my left,
and a hill strangled with vetch
to my right, orange soils
underfoot, and over it all
this same sky, everything

calm, very blue, hot,
the earth soaking up shadows, so that
it is all I can do to keep my own
walking before me into Marseilles
to stretch out at last over the foul

iridescent scums of the harbor,
over the great turnings and scatters of baitfish,
wheelings of fire, the sun
in billions flung back; and then
beneath it all, something

much larger, a slow
closing in from the sea, not mine
but a cloud's shadow, had the sky
not been as I think of it clear;
and the green milky stare of that eye looking up

through all the insane skitter and dash
of the schoolfish into the calm
bright power of the day
where I, having myself
only that moment arrived,

look down through my shadow
into the harbor of Marseilles,
look down at the long fish-shape of darkness
staring back; and I breathe
in no hurry at all.

The Harbor

My shadow swims before me
over the dry, fiery soils
until at last it cools itself

on the stone wharves, stretches
over the sea which has crept inshore
to become the harbor,

at its edges golden
with long drifts of pollen, thickening
into wracks and stoneworts,

into the slow mass
of the stone itself,
the land rising behind me

as if the sea had stolidly
heaved itself up
into the long swells of foothills,

mountains, into the whole
cresting ridge of the continent
which breaks to the North, bears

down on me, slowly
ebbs, at my feet
becomes the harbor, swells

and subsides
like breathing.

The Disconnections

When suddenly he took, whom I had sought
in my endless trolling back and forth
off Cape Bianca (froth
of bonito boiling
at sardines on the quarter, brake
and plunge of pelicans, off the bow
the huge cloud shadow
of the manta, the stony sea
shattering on the Santa Helena reefs,
and then the black fin
trailing the rigged *balao*, the cobalt bill
thrusting up from the wake, the line

unclipping from the right
outrigger, running loose)
I waited and struck
into the living shock and weight
of sea and sailfish; and at
the hookbite the sheer silver of him
leaped and leaped, the great fin
for an instant billowing
with purple light; and then

he broke away, the line end writhing
far astern, the big rod
springing back; whereupon
I reeled in and sat
stunned, to imagine his stunned
and panicked seaward flight,

the snapped line snaking
at his flank; and remembered

what in fact had been too brief
in the true light of the afternoon
to have truly recollected
with much in the way of faith, except
for the usual conviction
out of evidence: my hands
loosening on the rod, my heart

giving a little, salt crystals
grainy on my lips, my wondering
how it might have been, this time
to have brought him flaring and wallowing
in iridescences of spray boatside,
wide-gilled and azure, shimmering,
gaffed him in and lashed him down
astern, swathed him in damp sacking
against the sun. And even earlier,

heading out to sea, sighting
along the thread of current
to the oyster wharf diminishing
astern I saw the black girl

standing on a heap
of shells, waving, though not
to me, crumpling

a red hibiscus blossom
in her hand, until

the headland rose
between us; and felt again
the irrupt quickening, my body
urgent to cherish its express
knowledge of loss: girl

with flower, white
and distant flowering of the sea,
the great fish shining
in mid-air, all of it
risen or fallen
to improbable form,

though none of it
in any true or final nature
of the evidence (except perhaps
for the salt which on my tongue remains
a taste I cannot subdue, seem never
to have forgotten).
Days later

and ashore again I take
to cover, and at night
fall into something like sleep
on something like an incandescent sand,
prepared against the dry inclemencies
of loss, worry

the disconnections
in the considerable excess
of my way, consider
what has torn loose from me or breaks away
and then goes on as if
we had never touched and for
the moment caught
and held: I dream
of the bloodshock in the beautiful
pelagic bodies against mine, as if—
at least in the saltless dream as if—
each were required to be taken
as some shining, vigorous extrusion
of the sea. Here,

in the close dream
which the body bears,
out of the whole repertoire
of memory, I sense the slow

movement which conceals itself (headland
rising, the fish
suspended in its leap) and find
that what is small and far away
exhausts my sight (over the sea
which scarcely moves
and even as I say it
becomes more still,
an inclusion of gulls

hovers). And what
of all the congenerate shapes
a body makes most clearly moves
is the shadow of the girl sweeping
the white stone of the wharf from one
side to the other of her, power
of the circling light by which
I have come to yearn
for all that is pastless
and disjunct (slow

clasp of the strangler fig
shaping itself to the warm bole
of the palm; huge
flowering corpus of the sea,
whatever is made of the caught
and leaping body by what
bears in on it: infold of water,
salt or sun, the sea
shaping itself
to the bone's
mandrel). Here,

in the dream,
where all my people are,
stunned valencies loosed
to the toils of the assimilation,
I stand among the white waves
of the stones which root

in the vacuoles of the graves
and bloom with oleander
and hibiscus. Here I breathe

the salt air of the slow season,
which of what might be
exhausts only the part,
and call on myself again to dream
on this ten-thousandth night without
amendment, to make of it all again
the generosity beyond the need,
extend without correction

the vision: how it might be
that in the end we come together, red
flower, fish and girl, volume
of our being here embraced,
and all that stood between us
in the dazzling, translucid sea-light,
union of particles
beyond all series, never
so light as then, the earth
closed on itself and
centered, gravid
with bodies, trembling
to give birth.

Port Cities

I awaken on midwatch,
seeing by night vision
in the red light of the bridge,
the carrier steaming through darkness
at dead center on my scope,
the slow sweep trailing the green
fading fluorescences of headlands
behind it. And there is nothing

I can see by staring out
into that unreceptive and un-
tongued night *out there*, those
crashes of head-on water
at the bows, crestings
astern, only the slight
hiss and phosphorescences of wake;
but mostly darknesses
of sea and sky, though there

on the scope is the bright
proof of France, say, or
Gibraltar, the soft landshadow
curling itself around the green dazzle
at the heart of the compass rose.

And I feel the earth rising
beneath the sea, the sea itself
rising, the ship giving itself
upward, and the sky bearing down
onto the chill, red-lighted bridge.

I make it out as best I can:
I watched then from the red light of the bridge
out into the darkness, willing
by a greater outright substance of desire
than I have ever known
for light to come;
and to remember this

is to undertake as I have done
this measure,
this fixed distance from the center
around which the green
translucencies of after-image
persist, but wider
than reality, so that the true
bearing lies always
at their centers.
And it is after all

not so far behind me as I feared
when I thought to fear it,
seeing how today, in Vermont,
with me sitting outside my house
in broad daylight in the green shade
of the big California poplar,
watching Ray Fontaine plow up
his meadow, yellow
bursts of dandelions, blue
windstreaks of the cornflowers, white
foam of Queen Anne's Lace

borne down by the plowblade
into blue earth,

it so readily persists, nothing
in it of the landbound spill
of yellow light over the hay meadow,
the wavering of dry heat
along the road,
or the circle of shadow under
the silvery shaking poplar leaves,

but given rise to twenty-five years
and six thousand miles later and away
by no clear power of the sea (though once
this was the sea) *and everything
wrong for it:* the planet dry
and steady beneath me, the air
heavy with the smell of turned
soil and cows and tractor fumes
this silvery light, myself even

wrong for it, and yet
having it stir there, that hitch
at heart, that joy
in those cities in the washed mornings
rising before me from the bellies of the green seas,
at true bearing
in the eye of the alidade,
and still, and powerfully sleeping.

In those mornings came the headlands,
then Lisbon, Barcelona, Marseilles,
first pale light on the hilltops, the tops
of trees, tall
buildings, some slight
heave to the deck, perhaps, the screws

idling, the huge
turquoise upheaval of the wake
impossibly, perfectly straight
to far out from where in the night
we had begun our slow
run towards the lights of those cities
burning deep beneath the horizon, but ready
to rise like stars as we rode in
upon them; and the green harbors
curling away to each side
of the cutwater, like the soft
turning of sod.

After the necessary darknesses,
in the joyous instant of the recognition,
when the sun has at last risen
beyond the last possibility of light
truly suited to the eye,

when I am alone, the long
radiant streets narrowing away from me
in all directions, the currents

of the night roaring
far overhead,
in the long power of the long reflectionless day,
even here in Vermont, far from the sea,
I try imagining at the round heart of the earth
which bears the great cities,
a green like meadow grass, like the shadows
beneath pines; or that I am walking

down streets where, in the first of the morning,
having just arrived from the sea,
I am alone, the only one for hours
to take a breath or to watch
the bright sweep of the sky. At night
by the red light I imagine,
I try remembering the names of the trees
and flowers of those cities. At night
I wonder why it should be

we double in this manner on ourselves,
arrive from seaward, believing in the land
we have never seen before,
wishing for all the cities of the world
to rise before us like stars,
for the earth from which they rise
to lighten itself, become
one huge translucency, to free
the huge coil of its single root
to that recollection of light
we love so, which is our burden.

Poem on My Birthday

*"Do you feel in your heart
that life has turned out
as once you expected it?"* —R. P. Warren.

1

On those nights when I cannot sleep,
when my wife cries out beside me,
unsettled in sleep,
and I look from the bedroom window, and see
the pale upward-shedding of light
which precedes the moon,

often I permit myself
something in the nature of dream,
in which, trying to call out a woman's name,
I whisper merely *you! you!*

And often then my wife,
who is beautiful in sleep,
will stir, open her eyes, turn
towards me so that for a moment I
can imagine her awake, though because

this is in the order of dream,
and because in the dreams which I permit myself,
I permit no voice beyond my own,
she never speaks. *You!*

I cry, and
turn my head on the pillow, change
the dream, see
in the cleft of the orange curtains
the moon rise into a cloud,
which act I choose to take
as a sign, having
no other understanding.

2

The moon trembles and hesitates
in the low clouds near the peak.
As usual the light
is arriving with difficulty.
Still, I wait, and patiently;
beside me my wife—
most resembling what most
I have understood myself
to wish to love—

is herself dreaming of light,
though a greater urgency of it,
as in the whole shimmering upwards

of a day, the bright
shrub of the sun
shimmering upwards
from the sea

3

On those nights when I cannot sleep,
the moon slowly discloses itself to me;
and waiting for the full grace of its light,
I must trust my eye to see
over the dark belly of what
I have taken to be the world,
never ceasing to believe

that with the moon risen
the whole round light of the sky
will suddenly become
what suddenly I know myself
to have always believed in
as the sky

4.

Do I feel in my heart
that life has turned out
as once I expected it?
May I speak
into the sky? Is the sky
any less or more
silent than the cold air
of these rooms of this
old house which surrounds
this bed in which I am
awake in which
some people must
have died? and if
I speak into the general silences
as I have spoken and it
has been permitted; and if
I may ask what it is that is spoken
by the river among the boulders
at its edges, expecting

neither myself nor the river nor anyone
to answer, then why

may I not without awkwardness
address myself
to the bright stone
of the moon? And do,
for that is the need
as I have taken it to be:

Moon, I see you there,
just risen, just
free of the mountain,
just free of the unsettled
stone of the peak,
to which you have lent
some little light.

5

The moon, having risen,
is about to set.
How cool the moonlight, how decorously it drifts
in the high feathery ridges
of the pines, how it snows
down onto the fields
and the yards!
By moonlight

came here for the first time
to this place and have not left.
By moonlight once
walked clear down Ripton Mountain
out to find
my wife, who had
not left, though
wanted to; by moonlight faced

then as now into my own most
unbecoming neither
warm nor generous
desire. Truth is, O Moon,
I was not up to snuff: ask who I was

I did not offer back, indeed,
drew back from all
the humble and particular
conjunctions: empty
potencies of light, pale shapes
the body makes, though everything

hinges on it! *Moonset:* watch
the shadow draw back
on itself. O

silences I take to be
reprisal!

6

White run of the yard
down to the garden,
pale stubble of trees, the sky
scarcely lighter than
the trees, Orion grazing
the horizon, starlings grazing on
so far as I can tell plain ice:
I see the first moon of the new year rise

from out of the pines, swell
coldly into the sky
trailing the torn roots
of its fires; snow dusts
on the cedars and the pines.
In deepest winter, this far in the year,

what I wish for most is that
the white trees of the spring
might shortly root
in what I find it possible to think of,
even in this season, as
these passionate, these
reasonable soils.

7

In the Beginning, and not
for the first time, the moon

rose and fell, and that was all; except,
it is true, there was the first night
of the first dream, in which

each heard the other call out
to the other. Then, in the morning,
in the full light of the fresh sun,
in all the gorgeous outcry of that light,

neither could recall, both
having kept between them
careless watch. And that

was all, and near
enough the truth
to set it acting.

8

Speak to the Moon: O Moon,
I am grateful my wife sleeps
so that I, openly and without embarrassment,
may speak to you in this other voice,
knowing I cannot be heard
nor persuaded from retrieval. I do

not often now nor much
swell with the old abundancies, the room
is always all but cold enough; sweat

ices over, and the breath between us
whitely blooms. Moon,

I have never made my peace
with distances.

9

I endure the lateness in which the moon
is only just beginning its decline,
in which the snow is just beginning
to display shadows:

so distant before me
that it becomes one darkness
with that beneath the pines
is the last reach of the shape I make

when I stop light.

10

I walk my trail backwards through
the snow all night, circling
back, doubling on myself: and wing-marks
everywhere. When morning comes,

light breaks through the bright
veils of the curtains. I think of this

as I lie here in the bed
a whole night sleepless, amazed
that in so cold and bone-lit a regime,
the weather-fear upon me, I
still consent to be led

in the struggle with
the Angel; may, in fact,
be lost; though not, in fact,
so deeply I
will not survive.

11

Beyond height, not
overhead, but simply
out there, light

springs up, the earth swims
in great encircling currents of light.
Until now,
except for the moon circling
and circling this cold
notion of center, it has been
nearly the blackest night ever
to blind me; for the first time
I think it possible
this is a dream I have not made myself.

II

Earth Tremor, the Sky at Night

In the smoky light-mix of the sky
above Los Angeles,
over the frond-bursts
of the canyon palms
the night is ready: fog moves in

and I look up to see
what I think are stars,
swollen bodies of saffron light
exceedingly too near,
as it turns out, as always in fact

no more than some bright diffusion
of the literal, this time
streetlights on the far rim of the canyon
seen through fog; not far away
the seabed dives beneath

the raw edge of the continent,
the house shivers, my reflection
doubles in the window,
and I look out, steady myself to see,
and the weather lifts and thins

so that everything out there reveals itself
in all the common logic of display,
that static magnitude of true light
such as the true stars at true
distance dwindle to, such

as the companion body dwindles to
once its weathers clear.

The Fragonard, the Pietà, the Starry Sky

1

I am happiest here on the street,
walking with this woman, my hand on her arm,
the sun bright with forsythia,
the great subterranean waves of the granite
breaking in the park;

but in the galleries, less happy,
less happy in the private light
where she abandons me to stand
on the far side of the room
to see the child Virgin in the early practice
of her art, threading a needle,
the rosy candle suffuse
in her fingers,
her face white, shadowless, intent.

2

I am amazed at the brilliance
of the Northern palette,
the alizarins, madders, lakes,
bright in the folds of the saints' robes,
ceruleans clear as shallows
over a white ground.
But not far on,

among the jewels, white stocks,
blacks and umbers of the merchants,
I feel a slow darkening, a roiling

of greens and blues, shadows
taking place.
And before long
I cannot look anywhere

without wanting to bolt
from the bored, black-stockinged whores
on their sallow bed, the rose nipples
of the Polynesian girl, her basket
of scarlet berries,
the convulsed cypress that strains
to the star, the lion ravenous
in the midst of a cold, viridian foliage.
When it is time for me to leave

she walks with me halfway to the doors,
turns back, and I look after her:
small and bright in a blue shirt, climbing
the long stairs,
back to the company of the saints.

3

I go out
into the shining street
and stand for a moment at the fountain,
the spray beading on the light hairs of my hands.

And I do not know what to make
of all this joyous, watery display,

seeing I am alone again.
So that when I walk back home
the city becomes the spinning-out
of the shadow from whose foot I grow,
and which persists.

4

I awaken, not knowing I have slept,
and the sun, which all night
was locked in the stone of New York City,
breaks loose, becomes fire,
grows so intense a heart that to look into it
is to go blind in a white dazzle. Then,

little by little,
the sun wearies of this burning and permits
the city to rise and cover it.
And at nightfall I witness this descent of fire,
and the rising of the streets to meet it,

and I feel myself again
at the root of the contorted tree,
at the boundary between the light storm
and the static rock.
And in the night, when it finally comes,
I see how the sun allows the shadow,
and contains it,
and cry out, therefore, impatient

for the star that is hope,
the sunset radiance that is
the body's eagerness.

5

Later, at this achromatic business,
I tell myself it must be that her face
answers to all the names in the world,
that I do not know
how the body should be written,
in what flush or ruddiness,
or how to make the hand
translucent with fire.

I try remembering in which gallery
two cupids, spirits of departed lovers,
embraced in a shattered sarcophagus,
bereft companions fluttering tearfully about,
while the smiling Genius of Love
lighted the scene with a nuptial torch.
I take it to be

the law of measure that applies,
love's progress, as in the panels of the Fragonard:
on the white fields of the walls
a melee of doves and flowers,
the voices of the youthful lovers,

so fair, so fresh, so likely to endure,
abounding to their pink destruction.

But the one time that my hand
moved to her breast, she turned from me;
and I interrupt myself to consider that,
to break the great quotidian joy of Fragonard,
then to imagine her alone before
the paintings, fixed

by the severities of the *pietà*,
astonished at the blue callosities,
the wounds, the blue body
of the Christ
which nothing of moth and worm
shall have to heritage; above all

desiring to be
of that sheer power of love and grief
as Mary, the Magdalen, the John
who shudder with tears, the black holes
of their mouths raised to the dead Face,
their eyes, hands, arms to one another,
bellowing, lovely, loud with grief
forever into the intractable
white field of the sky *come back!*

Van Gogh Prophesies the Weathers of His Death

One morning I will awaken
out of the dream of which I did not see the end
to the visible logic of this sky
clouded and threshing with great stars,
and find myself unable to close my eyes,
staring, helpless, into the slow,
opening heart of the sun. And then
as the terrible light widens
and comes finally to bloom
in the fiery shades of the cypresses,
it will seem to me the young trees are moving,
as if to a light wind.

Or it may be
that one night, alone
in the spaces of the house my body makes,
the last partition of the heart attained, and all
the clocks gone out,
I call out, and am not heard,
and wait for a little, and then call out again,
in no despair, thinking I see the moon
move in the radiant clouds which are
the cypresses. And for a time, at least,
at least for the measure of this time,

I do not die, I am not
entirely unhappy, thinking
into the enormous roar and uprush of the light,
the dream of light that has possessed the work,
how nothing has troubled

the beauty of the world, not
the bare eye of the night
nor the eye's first gathering,
not the first rising of the breath,
nor the last,
not even the dream without color
on which my eyes will close,
for which I have this long time
prepared myself, whispering
into my dry teeth, moved
to the strangeness: how
after all the turbulent fluidities of fire
I have seen the sky to be,
it should have been
the one thing most like light, the way
the slim branches of the young trees,
themselves nothing like light,
with the wind among them turned and brightened.

Mahler Waiting

I wait at noon in the summer house
at Mäiernigg, the distant
voices of children unbearable,
the scraping together of oak leaves, a dog
which has been barking
for hours. That is all. I am

exhausted. *Dear wife, I have not been
alone!* The afternoon
is exhausted: piano salesmen
bawling over the fences, Wagner
struggling with his coat; Bruckner,
fat pork butcher of a man; Burckhardt,
who assured me that one morning
his eyes would stay shut, and then
he would be forever blind; Schoenberg,
riddler; Pfitzner, your particular
fool; and Wolf, who is dead

in that dead silence that follows
the stroke on the muffled
drum; finally, the child
who is dead, and whose name
I will not speak *(how night descends
to smother even the holiest
of days!)* When I consider how
once I believed in the blue
flower, the indeterminate
desire; how I wished
that every man might know

by what intent I spoke
to him; how I imagined
that in the end I should have waited out
this air, cold with the coppery smell
of zinnias—dear wife, when I am dead
I will call back to you
now the danger is past! Now

I spend a quiet afternoon.
I am almost well again. I eat
with appetite. I mean to be
in perfect health. But the silence
of this afternoon is an
intolerable thing, when I
consider how by any measure *(breath,*
eyeblink, heartbeat) I hurtle in
the vast, stellar agitations, by my small
weight the very planet
perfected in orbit. And I

imagine what might be its sudden
catastrophic lurch at my least
miscalculation, shift of weight: the clashing
of boulders, trees battering one
another, floods, tornadoes, the fires
bellowing outward
from the deep heart of the world!
I want to cry out

Mozart! Mozart! as if it were
already the end. Soon enough

I will hear the footsteps
of the servant who brings me tea,
her stertorous
breathing. This place
is high on the hillside,
over the house. I look down

through oak-leaves
at the roof. Sometimes it seems to me
I am falling: for all my vigilance
I am never clear how it begins,
I never know
if I have stumbled, been pushed, leaped.
There is not much more
to say: it begins with falling,

the calling-out in mid-air, the cool
choice of stance: flight, or the posture
that will drive the thighbones up
into the heart. In this vision
I am waiting for the bright explosion
which never comes. Well, dear wife, however
Death and Genius arrogate my hand,
I am hungry,
it is time.

I watch my fingers smoothing
the white cloth, the table
is perfectly laid, everything in high
order: the knives

gleaming in place, the hard,
cold bellies of spoons, everything
fixed in utter space.

For Mozart, from the Beginning

So magnified with new light
as to have become estranged
from the simple work, the song
continues itself. And since

from the blue radiance of the beginning
it rose into these minor volumes of the light
the greater we dream of
must from the beginning have contained;

and since the implacable light of the new sun
shone down upon the earth in which everything
was true, since then—
in the line of those few

who, seeing clearly by this light
have been somehow informed to choose
to love us and we have perhaps
loved back—there has been this one

to whom we might, with something
like the ease of instinct, speaking with something
like joy and in the fullness
of praise, have found it possible

to have cried aloud, but did not, that he
is indeed and always loved, who,
against all amulet and recipe, against
the cold gratuities of the subjectless,

seized in the real and made to flash forth
the mute transparencies
of matter, continued
the Creation, his heart so new,

boundless and unaltered, so
inhabited by beatitude,
as to have occasioned us to rise
from the regions of dissemblance toward one

another; and this despite
the effronteries of the disparate
body, sad goiter
of the other, because

his heart, and precisely by power
of the disaccord, from the first
instant of the first
spasm of light, prime turbulence, chord

of the Beginning, intent
on the immaculate bond of the ensemble, free
to cherish the light, beat, measured itself
and never otherwise gave voice

to the gorgeous numbers
of the increate sensation,
the disinterested poetry
of the source.

Vivaldi in Early Fall

O this is what it is to be
Vivaldi, in September, in my
forty-eighth year, the pines
just beginning to sing
on the hillsides, the rivers
coloring with the first rains
(which are, as usual, precisely
on time). And there is also

this young girl, who, each year,
I bring into my mind,
making it to be that if she knew
by what measure I considered her,
she would turn and look at me and smile,
thinking, "It is the priest again,
the one with red hair, who is said
to make music, and who—as every year—
has gone a little sweetly crazy,
and I think he may love how I am today
in my blue dress." And she
is right. In September I am moved
to the melancholy theme: I like to make the cello
sing with the pines, be on the verge
of the thunderously sad. And, as always,
at this time I would like to make the melody

go on forever, but cannot, being cursed
to disdain my narrow lusts
and sorrows. I have never said
that with me an innocent angel

is alone at work: it may be
I exercise the murderous grace.
But in September, the face of God
passes through my walls to show me
how the motion of song sleeps
at the center of the world, as, indeed,
among the Angels, innocent of time. I hear

at this time every year the voice that loves me
crying out *return, return!* and I do, I round
on the beginning in full belief:
and the girl is gone, having never breathed
as I breathe, in the weary
exactitude of matter. The song
stops at the certain moment
of its growth. It is
the truth of me, not any lie
that I imagine, and I
can do nothing with it. Still,

it is autumn, and over the whole world
the air resumes its liveliness; and I,
Vivaldi, possessed of love and confidence
in measure wonderful to me, I seek
to magnify the text: *viola, bassoon, cello,*
it is as if the trees have broken into song,
and the song roots, blossoms, thrusts
deep toward the still center, overspreads
the sky like a million breathing leaves.

Notes

Notes

In "Thinking of the Garden," the cry attributed to Yuan Chen is from "Three Dreams at Chiang-ling," translated by William H. Nienhauser and included in *Sunflower Splendor: Three Thousand Years of Chinese Poetry*, eds. Liu and Lo (New York: Anchor Press/Doubleday, 1975), p. 216.

In "The Garden," lines 1–6 are adapted from C. S. Lewis's summary description of the garden of *The Romance of the Rose* in *The Allegory of Love* (New York: Oxford University Press/Galaxy, 1958), p. 119.

The image of "the dark-enclosing vault / of the dead box turtle's shell" which occurs in "The Guardian of the Lakes at Notre Dame," has recently and increasingly seemed to me one I have encountered elsewhere, though I have searched for it without discovering a source. At the time I wrote the poem the image seemed my discovery, and so it remains. But if it should turn out that I have in fact remembered rather than discovered it, I ask the pardon and tolerance of the poet whose property I may have plundered.

In "Bog Plants," the line "sitting alone / which is the beginning of error" is borrowed from Robert Penn Warren, who has kindly consented to my use of it.

Frank O'Malley, my late and beloved teacher at Notre Dame, taught me that the body is weak "on the side which does not lean upon the world," a phrase that occurs in "After Thirteen Years."

In "The Fragonard, the Pietà, the Starry Sky," the phrase at the end of part 4 is a recasting of Van Gogh's remark in one of his letters to Theo to the effect that often he cries out "impatient for the star that is hope, the sunset radiance that is the soul's eagerness."

And, finally, in "Mahler Waiting," I am generally indebted for certain phrases, remarks, and the shape of the initial anecdote to Alma Mahler's memoirs. "The blue flower" occurs in one of the lieder, and is acknowledged by Irving Babbitt as the symbol for romantic aspiration, "the indeterminate desire."

Other Titles in the Contemporary Poetry Series